D1626389

Experiments
with
MATERIALS

Isabel Thomas

a Capstone company — publishers for children

Raintree is an imprint of Capstone Global Library Limited, a company incorporated in England and Wales having its registered office at 7 Pilgrim Street, London, EC4V 6LB – Registered company number: 6695582

www.raintree.co.uk
myorders@raintree.co.uk

Edited by Holly Beaumont
Designed by Steve Mead
Picture research by Jo Miller
Production by Helen McCreath
Printed and bound in China

ISBN 978 1 406 29788 1
19 18 17 16 15
10 9 8 7 6 5 4 3 2 1

British Library Cataloguing in Publication Data
A full catalogue record for this book is available from the British Library.

Acknowledgements
We would like to thank the following for permission to re-produce photographs: Getty Images: National Geographic/James L. Amos, 17; Glow Images: ImageSource, cover (bottom), 15 (bottom); Science Source: Colin Cuthbert, 7 (bottom); Shutterstock: Africa Studio, 23 (top), Dean Fikar, 23 (bottom), Madlen, 10, michaeljung, 5, 28 (top), Pavel L Photo and Video, 7 (top), TRIG, 16

All other photographs were created at Capstone Studio by Karon Dubke.

We would like to thank Patrick O'Mahony for his invaluable help in the preparation of this book.

Every effort has been made to contact copyright holders of material reproduced in this book. Any omissions will be rectified in subsequent printings if notice is given to the publisher.

All the internet addresses (URLs) given in this book were valid at the time of going to press. However, due to the dynamic nature of the internet, some addresses may have changed, or sites may have changed or ceased to exist since publication. While the author and publisher regret any inconvenience this may cause readers, no responsibility for any such changes can be accepted by either the author or the publisher.

The publisher and author disclaim, to the maximum extent possible, all liability for any accidents, injuries or losses that may occur as a result of the information or instructions in this book.

Safety instructions for adult helper
The experiments in this book should be planned and carried out with adult supervision. Certain steps should **only** be carried out by an adult – these are indicated in the text. Always follow the instructions carefully.

The materials used in these experiments are safe to handle, unless you have a specific allergy (e.g. egg, page 11). Some everyday materials, such as vinegar, may irritate sensitive eyes or skin. It is recommended to wear eye protection when mixing materials. Wash your hands after each experiment. Never eat or drink anything used in your experiments, or use eating utensils for experiments.

Contents

Some words are shown in bold, **like this**. You can find out what they mean by looking in the glossary.

Why experiment?

Why can't we see the salt in the sea? Does hot chocolate *have* to be made with hot water?

Scientists ask questions like these. They work out the answers using **scientific enquiry** – and the really fun part is the **experiments**!

You can be a scientist by asking questions about the world and using experiments to help find the answers.

Follow these steps to work like a scientist

Ask a question.

Come up with an idea to test.

Plan an experiment.

What will you change?
What will you keep the same?
What will you measure?

Make a **prediction**.

Observe carefully.

Work out what the results mean.

Answer the question!

An experiment is a test that has been carefully planned to answer a question.

The experiments in this book will help you to find out more about **materials**, and what happens when you mix different materials together.

IS IT A FAIR TEST?

Most experiments involve changing something to see what happens. Make sure you only change one **variable** at a time. Then you will know that the variable you are testing is what made the difference. This is called a fair test.

⚠ **WARNING!** Ask an adult to help you plan and carry out each experiment. Follow the instructions carefully. If you see these signs, you will need to take extra care, or ask for adult help.

ADULT HELP

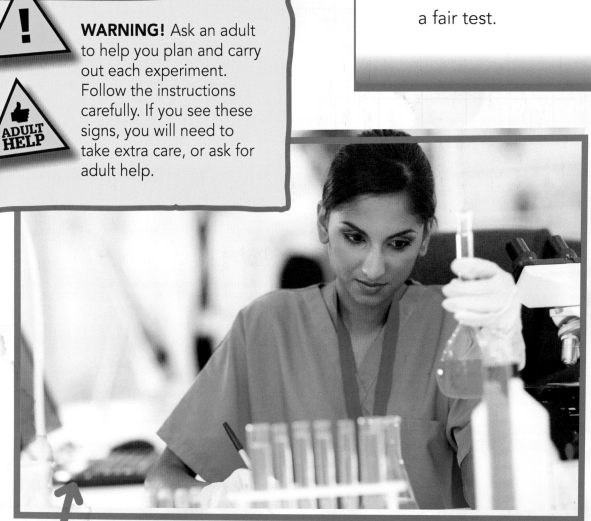

Get your eyes, ears, nose and hands ready! You'll need to observe your experiments carefully and record what you see, hear, smell and feel.

What are materials?

Everything you can see, touch, smell or breathe in is made of "stuff". To describe that "stuff", scientists use the word **materials**.

Most materials, such as air, rocks and cotton, are found in nature. People can invent new materials by mixing and changing natural materials. Plastic and concrete are **synthetic** materials.

SEE THE SCIENCE ⬇

Pick two materials and compare their **properties**. Are the materials **transparent** or **opaque**? Do they take in water or are they waterproof? Are they hard or soft? How many other properties can you think of?

Describing materials

When we describe materials, we often talk about the way they look or behave in different situations. "Waterproof", "bouncy", "shiny" and "see-through" are all properties.

Right for the job

Every material has a set of properties that makes it useful for certain jobs – and completely useless for others!

What would happen if you swapped the materials used for each part of this toy? Would it still fly?

REAL WORLD SCIENCE

Materials scientists study the properties of materials. They use their findings to sort materials into groups. They also design new materials, with the right combination of properties for certain tasks.

Knee pads

Knowing about properties helps us choose the right material for a job. This **experiment** will help you find the best fabric to protect your knees when you're scooting or skateboarding.

Equipment

- 10 x 15-cm (4 x 6-in.) strips of different fabrics (e.g. denim, polyester, cotton, jersey, wool, nylon, fleece, canvas)
- Cork sanding block
- Tacks or drawing pins
- Small wooden block
- Rough sandpaper

Predict: Which fabric will be the toughest? Which will be the weakest?

Method

1 Stretch a piece of fabric tightly around the sanding block, pinning it in place at the back.

2 Cut a piece of sandpaper, and wrap it around the small wooden block. Rub it along the fabric from top to bottom.

3 Keep rubbing in the same way, counting as you go. How many rubs until you can see the cork through the fabric? Record your result.

4 Repeat these steps with the other pieces of fabric. Record your results in a table, like the one below. Do your results match your prediction?

Fabric	Number of times rubbed with sandpaper before a hole appeared

 IS IT A FAIR TEST?

Rubbing wears the sandpaper down, as well as the fabric. To make it a fair test, use a new piece of sandpaper each time.

Conclusion

The toughest fabric is the one that withstood the highest number of rubs. This would be the best type of fabric to wear for protecting your knees when scooting or skateboarding.

What is a mixture?

Another set of **properties** describes how **materials** behave when you mix them with other materials. A **mixture** is made up of two or more materials. The materials in a mixture have not changed – they are just jumbled up together.

This is a mixture of different types of sweets.

Mixtures and solutions

If you mix a spoonful of mud into a jar of water, pieces of mud spread through the water, turning it brown. If you mix salt with water (like in the sea), the salt seems to vanish and the water still looks clear. Where does the salt go?

Salt **dissolves**. It breaks up into pieces so tiny that you can't see them any more. These tiny pieces spread through the water. This special type of mixture is called a **solution**.

If you tasted the solution, it would taste salty. A less yucky way to prove the salt is there is to pop a fresh egg into the jar before adding the salt. In fresh water, the egg sinks, but a solution with lots of salt in is **denser**, so the egg floats!

SEE THE SCIENCE ⬇

Mix these materials with water to find out which ones are **soluble** (dissolve) in water, and which ones are **insoluble** (don't dissolve) in water: salt, sugar, coffee granules, milk, gravy granules, baking soda, vitamin C tablets, washing up liquid, squash, cooking oil

 Do not taste or eat any of your mixtures, and pour them away afterwards so that no one else drinks them by mistake!

Dissolving detective

Can water keep **dissolving** a substance forever? Does the temperature of the water make a difference? Try these **experiments** to find out.

How many sugars?

Equipment

- Salt
- Sugar
- Baking soda
- Water from a cold tap
- Three jars (or glasses)
- Dark paper

- Measuring jugs
- Teaspoon
- Spoon for stirring

Method

1   Measure half a jug of water into each jar. Place them on a dark surface. This will help you to see if the substances have dissolved.

2   Measure salt into the first jar, a teaspoon at a time. Stir after adding each teaspoon. Does the salt dissolve?

3 Keep adding salt to the same jar, a teaspoon at a time. How many teaspoons can you add before it stops dissolving?

If you can see tiny specks of salt that don't dissolve after stirring, the water has dissolved as much salt as it can.

Predict: Will you be able to dissolve the same amount, more or less of the other substances in the same amount of water?

4 Repeat with the other jars, using sugar and baking soda. How many teaspoons can you add before they stop dissolving?

IS IT A FAIR TEST?

The **variable** you are changing is the **material** being dissolved. Make sure the volume and temperature of the water are the same in every jar. You'll find out why this is important in the next experiment!

Material	Teaspoons added before it stopped dissolving
Salt	
Sugar	
Bicarbonate of soda	

Record your results in a table like this.

5 **Analyse** your results. Was there a difference?

Find the solution

Does the temperature of the water change the amount of salt that **dissolves**? Carry out a second **experiment** to find out.

Equipment

- Salt
- Cold water
- Hot water
- Two jars or glasses
- Measuring jug

- Teaspoon
- Spoon for stirring

Method

1 Measure half a jug of water from the cold tap into one jar, and half a jug of water from the hot tap into the second jar.

Predict: Will warmer water dissolve more or less salt?

ADULT HELP
Ask an adult to check the water is not too hot before you use the tap.

2 Measure salt into the first jar a teaspoon at a time. Stir after each spoonful. How many teaspoons can you add before the salt stops dissolving?

3 Measure salt into the jar of warm water a teaspoon at a time. Stir after adding each teaspoon. How many teaspoons can you add before the salt stops dissolving?

4 **Analyse** your results. Did changing the temperature make a difference?

REAL WORLD SCIENCE

People heat water to make solutions such as coffee, tea, gravy and hot chocolate. The hot water helps the substances dissolve more quickly.

Conclusion

Some **materials** are **soluble** in water. This is a **property** of these materials. However, there is a limit to how much can dissolve. This is different for different materials. It also changes with the temperature of the water. When the water has dissolved all the material it can, we say the **solution** is saturated.

How can mixtures be separated?

You can always separate a **mixture** and get the original **materials** back. Mixing is **reversible**. Knowing the **properties** of each material in a mixture helps us work out how to separate them.

Separating solids

You could separate a mixture of sweets by picking out all the green ones. It would not be so easy to separate a mixture of flour and rice by hand, but you could sieve the mixture. Tiny pieces of flour pass through the sieve. Larger rice grains are left behind.

Combine harvesters have sieves inside. The part of the crop we want – the tiny grains – fall through the holes and are collected. The bits we can't eat are left behind, and dropped back on to the field.

The best way to separate a mixture depends on the properties of the materials. Lorries deliver a mixture of many different materials to recycling centres. Some of these materials are separated by hand. Blasts of air separate paper and card from heavier materials. Magnets are used to separate steel and aluminium cans.

Separating solids and liquids

What about a **mixture** of sand and water? You could filter the mixture. The tiny holes in filter paper let water through, but trap sand or soil.

Separating solutions

Sieving and filtering will not help you to separate **solutions**. The **dissolved** salt and the water can both pass through tiny holes. Instead, you can heat the water until it evaporates (turns into a gas and goes into the air). The salt will be left behind. The **water vapour** can be caught and cooled, so it changes back into water.

SEE THE SCIENCE ⬎

Fizzy drinks have a gas dissolved in them. The gas usually separates from the liquid slowly, escaping as tiny bubbles. You can speed this up by dropping a sugar cube into a bottle of fizzy drink. Bubbles of gas form quickly on the rough surface.

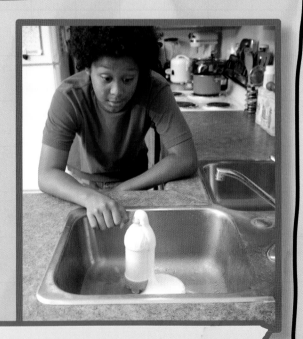

⚠ **!** Stand the bottle in a sink or in the garden when you do this!

Separating mixtures

Chromatography is another clever way to separate solutions. You can use it to investigate the mixtures of colours used to make brown sweets.

Equipment

- Large square of white filter paper, blotting paper or art paper
- Different brands of sweets with brown sugar shells
- Drinking straw
- Glass of water

Method

1   Put the square of paper on a flat, waterproof surface. Arrange the sweets evenly across the centre of the paper.

    Write down the names of all the sweets so that you know which is which.

2 Use the straw to put six drops of water on each sweet.

 IS IT A FAIR TEST?

The **variable** you are changing is the brand of sweet. Everything else should stay the same. Add the same amount of water to each sweet, and leave it for the same amount of time. Is it a fair test if each sweet is a different size and shape? How could you make your **experiment** fairer?

3 The drops of water should form a pool underneath each sweet. Leave your experiment for 5 to 10 minutes.

4 Look at the paper around each sweet. What do you see? Let the paper dry out. Draw a table to record your results.

Brand of sweet	Colours on paper after chromatography
M&Ms	
Minstrels	
Skittles	

5 **Analyse** your results. Did each brown sweet produce the same number of colours? Is there a difference between sweets made with artificial colours and sweets marked "no artificial colours"?

Conclusion

All dyes and colourings are a **mixture** of the primary colours – blue, yellow and red. Each dye is a different **material**. In this experiment, the brown colouring from different sweets **dissolved** in water. The **solution** travelled through the paper. The water could carry some colours further than others, so the colours were separated. This shows that "brown" is made up in many different ways.

The most **soluble** dyes are usually carried the furthest. Try the same experiment using sweets of different colours.

Changed forever

Scientists love mixing **materials** together to find out what happens. Some materials may form a **mixture** or a **solution**. Others **react** together to make completely new materials.

Add a teaspoon of bicarbonate of soda to water – it **dissolves** and forms a solution. Now add a teaspoon of bicarbonate of soda to vinegar. What signs are there that the bicarbonate of soda and vinegar are changing into new materials?

One of the new materials is a gas. You can collect it inside a balloon!

Heating mixtures

Some **irreversible** changes happen only when you add heat. A mixture of paper and air does nothing. But add heat, and the paper and air burn. They change into ash and gases. Burning is an irreversible change.

Baking is also an irreversible change. You can't change a cake back into flour, sugar, butter and eggs once it has been cooked.

Irreversible changes can be very useful. When a material burns, lots of energy is released. We use the energy from burning fuel to heat and light our homes, and to power machines.

SEE THE SCIENCE ↴

Some changes, or **reactions**, happen very quickly. Others are much slower. Leave an iron nail outside for a few days. The iron reacts with air and water, and changes into rust. The rust is a new material. You can scrape it off, but you can't separate it back into iron, water and air.

Sometimes we look for ways to stop or slow down changes. We paint iron to stop it from rusting, and we keep food in the fridge to slow down **decay**.

Plastic from a cow?

Irreversible changes can help scientists to make new **materials**, with different **properties**. **Experiment** with vinegar and milk to design a new material of your own.

Equipment

- ½ bottle each of four different types of milk (such as whole milk, semi-skimmed milk, skimmed milk, soya milk, rice milk or coconut milk)
- Jug
- White vinegar
- Small pan and heat source
- Spoon
- Sieve
- Wet wipes or old tea towel

Method

ADULT HELP

1 Ask an adult to heat half a bottle of whole milk gently. When the milk is warm (but not boiling), ask the adult to pour it into a jug.

2 Add two teaspoons of vinegar to the milk in the jug. Stir gently. What happens? Can you see any signs that the materials are changing?

3 After a minute, pour the contents of the jug through the sieve. What can you see in the sieve?

> Place a wet wipe or old tea towel over the base of the sieve. This will make the next step easier.

4 When the lumps are cool, gather the cloth and twist gently to squeeze out any remaining liquid.

5 Open up the cloth – you have made a ball of white material. How does it look, feel and smell? What happens when you squeeze it, shape it or bounce it? Record your **observations**.

EXPERIMENT 4

What happened?

When you mix together vinegar and warm milk, the **materials react** and change. A new material forms, called a polymer (like plastic).

6 Repeat steps 1 to 5 using a different type of milk each time.

> Put each plastic in a different container, labelled with the type of milk you used.

7 Leave the lumps to dry overnight, then try squeezing and bouncing them. How do they look, feel and behave now? Record your **observations** at each stage. Use a table like the one below, so it is easy to compare your results when the **experiment** is over.

Type of milk	Observations at stage 5	Observations at stage 7
Whole milk		
Semi-skimmed milk		
Skimmed milk		
Soya milk		

Predict: Will different milks produce different plastics, or will they all be the same?

IS IT A FAIR TEST?

You should only change one **variable** at a time – the type of milk. The amount of milk and vinegar should stay the same. Is it a fair test if the milk is heated to a different temperature each time? How could you make your experiment fairer?

8 **Analyse** your results. Were your predictions right?

Conclusion

Milk is full of protein. Adding vinegar causes the protein to stick together in long chains. These chains clump together, catching the fat in the milk like fish in a net. Different types of milk have different amounts of fat and protein in them. This is why they form "plastics" with different **properties**.

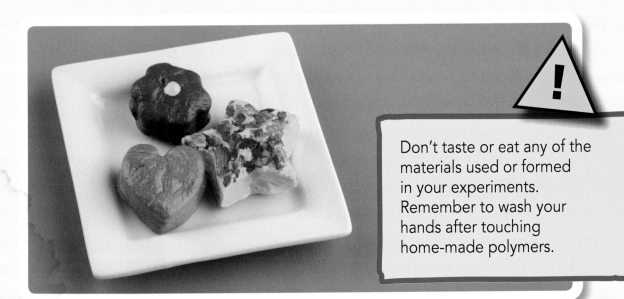

! Don't taste or eat any of the materials used or formed in your experiments. Remember to wash your hands after touching home-made polymers.

Your polymer will become very hard. Shape it while soft, then paint and varnish it once it has dried out.

Plan your next experiment

Experiments have helped you discover some amazing things about **materials**. Just like you, scientists carry out experiments to answer questions and test ideas. Each experiment is planned carefully to make it a fair test.

Scientists are finding out new facts all the time. Experiments also lead to new questions!

Did you think of more questions about materials? Can you plan new experiments to help answer them?

Being a scientist and carrying out experiments is exciting. What will you discover next?

YOU FOUND OUT THAT...

Materials have different physical **properties**, which make them suitable for different jobs.

Some materials can be mixed together. Others don't mix. Some materials form a **solution** when they are mixed. There is a limit to how much material can **dissolve** in a certain amount of water.

Mixtures can always be separated. Some are easier to separate then others. You can work out how to separate a mixture by thinking about the properties of the different materials in the mixture.

Materials have different chemical properties. If two materials **react** together, they are changed forever. The change is **irreversible**. This can be very useful when we want to create new materials.

WHAT NEXT?

Can you design an experiment to test how waterproof or stretchy different materials are?

Oil does not dissolve in water, but if you shake them together, they form a mixture called an emulsion. Plan an experiment to find out if adding salt or pepper to salad dressing helps this emulsion to stay mixed.

Experiment to find the best method of separating a mixture of salt and sand. Hint: Like in the Separating mixtures chromatography experiment, you will need to make a solution first!

There are other materials that have similar **properties** to vinegar. Scientists call these acids. Plan an experiment to find out if different types of acid (for example, lemon juice) make different milk plastics.

Glossary

analyse examine the results of an experiment carefully, in order to explain what happened

decay reactions that break down a living thing after it has died

density how heavy an object is for its size

dissolve become broken up into tiny pieces and spread through a liquid

experiment procedure carried out to test an idea or answer a question

insoluble does not dissolve (in a particular liquid)

irreversible can't be reversed, or undone

material what something is made of

mixture substance made by mixing materials together

observation noting or measuring what you see, hear, smell or feel

opaque does not let light pass through

prediction best guess or estimate of what will happen, based on what you already know

properties how a material looks or behaves

react change

reaction when two or more materials have an effect on each other, that causes them to change

reversible can be reversed, or undone

scientific enquiry method used by scientists to answer questions about the world

soluble dissolves (in a particular liquid)

solution mixture of a liquid and another substance, which has dissolved in the liquid

synthetic human-made

transparent lets light pass through; see-through

variable something that can be changed during an experiment

water vapour water that has changed into a gas

Find out more

Books

Big Book of Science Things to Make and Do, Rebecca Gilpin (Usborne, 2012)

Exploring Kitchen Science, The Exploratorium (Weldon Owen, 2015)

It's Elementary!: Putting the Crackle into Chemistry (Big Questions), Robert Winston (Dorling Kindersley, 2010)

Make it Change! Whiz Kid Science, Anna Claybourne (Raintree, 2014)

Websites

www.bbc.co.uk/bitesize/ks2/science/materials/changes_materials/play
Become a secret agent and investigate changes in materials on this BBC website.

www.bbc.co.uk/schools/scienceclips/ages/7_8/characteristics_materials.shtml
On this website, you can test different materials to find out about their properties.

Index